IT'S THE SEX, STUPID!

Don't Let TRUMP & the GOP Sex-Scandal US Again!

Donald Trump threatens to use Bill Clinton's sex scandal against Hillary Clinton during the 2016 presidential election. If Trump loses, the GOP will attack HRC's presidency any way they can and we'll be hearing the name Monica Lewinsky again.

Sooner or later, we'll be revisiting the national trauma of the late '90's when Republicans manipulated the country with a sex-scandal. Since the world continues to suffer the disastrous consequences to this day, we better learn from the past are we'll be doomed to repeat it.

IT'S THE SEX, STUPID! reveals how politicians use sex scandals to manipulate, blackmail and ultimately screw the public. It also contains a sampling of the satiric 1998 *"I Had Sex With Clinton, Too!"* petition, which my wife and I organized to protest the sexual-political insanity that had overtaken the country and led to President Bill Clinton's impeachment. This historic petition is a rare and racy example of democracy in action.

IT'S THE SEX, STUPID! is a prophylactic against sexually-transmitted STDs—*Sex-Scandal-induced Thought Distortions*—and will help inoculate and immunize the body politic against the sex-scandaling manipulations of Donald Trump and the GOP during this presidential election and beyond.

— I. J. Weinstock, 2016

IT'S THE SEX, STUPID!

Don't Let TRUMP & the GOP Sex-Scandal US Again!

I.J. Weinstock

IT'S THE SEX, STUPID!
Don't Let TRUMP & the GOP Sex-Scandal US Again!
By I.J. Weinstock

ISBN-13: 978-0-9829322-9-2

More information:

DreaMasterBooks@gmail.com
www.DreaMasterBooks.com

For Joy

who laughed, loved & protested with me
against the sexual & political hypocrisy
that consumed our country in the late '90's.

Contents

It's the Sex-Scandal, Stupid!

by I. J. Weinstock

Nearly 20 years ago, Republican politicians manipulated the nation with a sex-scandal, and the world continues to suffer the disastrous consequences to this day. Donald Trump threatens to use the Clinton sex scandals against Hillary Clinton during the 2016 presidential campaign. If we don't learn the lessons of the past, we're doomed to get screwed again.

Flashback

In 1998, a sex scandal consumed the country. Subpoenas. Grand Juries. A Special Prosecutor. Impeachment. The Republicans called it an "investigation." The Democrats denounced it as a "witch-hunt!" The news media counted the days of the "White House in Crisis" much the way it did when "America Was Held Hostage" by Iran 25 years earlier. Day 72...Day 133...Day 219... But this time the enemy was within.

1

Though public opinion polls made it abundantly clear that the majority of Americans didn't give a damn about the investigation, partisan politicians more interested in power than governing turned it into a political Armageddon and took the government hostage.

For two years, while the seeds of Islamic fanaticism took root, the most powerful nation on earth was obsessed with a stained blue dress. If not for those two years of sex scandal-induced insanity, the world might look very different today.

Sex and the War on Terror

It's not often discussed by polite pundits and partisan politicians, but sex plays a central role in the War on Terror. Where would Islamic terrorists get suicide bombers if they didn't promise them a paradise of sexual fulfillment provided by 72 virgins? But fanatical Moslems aren't the only ones who are crazy when it comes to sex. Just look at how we went nuts during the Clinton sex scandal. That blue dress became our country's number one priority. Instead of taking the terrorist threat seriously and getting Osama Bin Laden, our Republican-led Congress tried to impeach President Clinton.

In an alternate universe in which we weren't so sex-crazy, the scandal gets no traction, President Clinton is free to govern and we kill Bin Ladin. The 9/11 plot is uncovered. The Twin Towers are still standing. The terrorist threat isn't blown up into a War on Terror in which we invade and occupy Muslim countries and destabilize the world.

Instead, we were manipulated by a sex scandal, suffered 9/11, went to war in Afghanistan and Iraq, and threw gasoline on the embers of Islamic fanaticism that eventually spawned Al Qaeda and ISIS. Makes you wonder if we're as crazy as the Islamic terrorists about sex? Just in a different way.

Fiddling While the World Burns

In 1998, the Clinton sex scandal consumed the country. The media fanned the flames for ratings and the government (particularly the Republican-controlled Congress) fiddled as Washington and the world burned.

While the most powerful nation on earth was on a *panty hunt* and its leader the target of a new *"Un-American Affairs Committee,"* Saddam Hussein defied the UN, the Balkans became a powder-keg, the Asian financial bubble burst, Russia teetered on the brink of economic and political chaos, India and Pakistan detonated nuclear weapons, and on and on. Perhaps most tragically, the American people's business—whether tobacco regulation, Social Security reform, or the future of health care—was ignored as partisan political war raged.

What could patriotic Americans do? How could citizens protest the sexual-political insanity that had overtaken the country? If the public opinion polls were having no impact on the powers-that-be, perhaps something more shocking was needed.

Fighting Sexual Hypocrisy with Sexual Fantasy

During the hysteria of the Clinton sex scandal, my wife, Joy, and I wanted to protest the sexual-political insanity that had overtaken the country. We decided to fight sexual hypocrisy with sexual fantasy!

We were inspired by the classic film "Spartacus" starring Kirk Douglas as the leader of a doomed slave revolt against Imperial Rome. In the climactic scene, the victorious Roman general demands that Spartacus be turned over to him. In a heroic act of defiance, the captured slaves demonstrate their loyalty and protect their leader by each declaring, "I am Spartacus!"

What if we did an *I am Spartacus!*? What if, as a demonstration of support and solidarity, we literally "got into bed" with the President? What if, as an act of political theater protesting the hypocrisy of the investigation, we actually confessed to having sex with President Clinton? And what if we created a petition of hundreds, maybe even thousands, of confessions and handed them over to the Independent Counsel, Kenneth Starr, who was investigating the President?

And so the *"I Had Sex With Clinton, Too!"* petition was born. We launched a primitive website and sent out a press release—*"New Political Website Invites Public to Have Sex with the President to Save the USA!"*

The Wall Street Journal wrote, "A new website mocks Starr's probe into Clinton's private life by urging people to file imaginary 'confessions' that 'I had sex with Clinton, too!'"

The St. Louis Post-Dispatch began an editorial about the website with, "If you support Bill Clinton, it's time to get in bed with him..."

ABCNews.com ran a feature story with the headline, "Jump in Bed with the President! Web Site Protests Clinton Scandal '90's-Style."

The Response

We heard from people from all over the country who felt as we did, understood what we were trying to do, and wanted to join the protest.

> *...I LOVE IT!!! This is a GREAT website!!! This is so CATHARTIC!!!...*
>
> *...Yes, we all did (HAVE SEX WITH CLINTON). If we can do anything to stop this bullshit, count us in!*
>
> *...CONGRATULATIONS!!!! At last—sanity in total absurdity. How can I help fuel this petition from Atlanta?*

...WELL DONE! I am glad to see other people annoyed with the media coverage of this ludicrous affair (no pun intended} when there are more important things on which we could focus our attentions. Kudos for thinking this up.

...Ken Starr is conducting such a massive perversion of justice that I am thinking guerrilla tactics like yours are in order!!

...Thanks a ton. It was good clean (and not so clean) fun, and finally gave me a chance to tell my whole story. What a release!

...HURRAH! for this cyber protest demonstration! Just what we need to rid ourselves of the trashy Starr investigation! How silly we must look to the rest of the world. Maybe we deserve it to wake us up to the corruption of using sex scandals for political manipulation games.

...Please add my name to the rolls of those who are "in bed with the president." Ask special prosecutor Kenneth Starr if he would like to interview me, as well. I'm sure I can find some juicy tidbits to share with him. Thanks for letting me vent my frustration with this whole mess!

...Hope it becomes the virtual million wo/man march on Washington.

...This investigation into the president's sex life is the most absurd thing I've ever seen in my entire life. Don't we have more important things to worry about in this country? It just shows our national obsession as well as discomfort with human sexuality.

...Thanks. I had a lot of fun telling all. But even more, I'm just glad to stand up for and participate in what freedom really means.

*...I believe that laid politicians are happy politicians, and happy politicians make (re)productive governments. That's why I had sex with the President! And that why I encourage ALL of my friends and colleagues to do the same, and to chant along on the White-House Cyber Lawn...
"Save the Government! F#@k the President!"*

The Confessions

The confessions started rolling in—at first a trickle, then a stream and ultimately a flood—nearly a thousand in all. Their humor and creativity far surpassed our expectations. More literary than graffiti. And what surprised us was what was confessed. They were more original, satirical and entertaining than anything we could have imagined. There was also something uniquely American about the freedom embodied in this X-rated petition.

IT'S THE SEX, STUPID!

Outraged Americans Protest Impeachment Probe
X-Rated Petition Uses Sex Fantasies to Protest Political Hypocrisy—
Hundreds Confess to Having Sex with Clinton

Los Angeles, 1998—Since public opinion seems to be having little effect on Congress' headlong rush to impeachment, some frustrated Americans are resorting to shock tactics to get their message to Washington in ways that cannot be ignored.

The "I Had Sex With Clinton, Too!" website has organized a petition comprised of more than 500 sexually explicit confessions from Americans who are so outraged by Starr's investigation, they've "gotten in bed" with the President and confessed that they, too, have had sex with Bill Clinton.

For the past several months, Jerry Weinstock and Joy Mitchell, the Los Angeles-based creators of the website, have invited people to protest the sexual and political hypocrisy of the Starr investigation by confessing their own imaginary sexual affairs with Bill Clinton.

"Hypocrisy is a polite term for lying," Weinstock said. "And everyone involved is guilty of hypocrisy, especially the President's accusers. We are outraged by the politicians' putting their partisan self-interests ahead of the country. They swore under oath to represent the people, and by ignoring the will of the people as well as the people's business, they've lied under oath, too. No one's hands are clean."

"Sometimes, you have to fight fire with fire," Mitchell added. "We've chosen to fight political and sexual hypocrisy with sexual fantasy! The "I Had Sex With Clinton, Too!" petition is meant to shock us back to our senses. We hope Congress gets the message and stops this destructive, partisan impeachment process."

When asked if their X-rated petition went beyond the bounds of decency and wasn't downright obscene, Weinstock replied, "This whole episode is obscene. Let's face it—as a nation we've gone crazy.

The media counts the days of the "White House in Crisis" much the same way it did when America was held hostage by Iran almost 20 years ago. And tragically, once again America is being held hostage. Only this time, the enemy is within!"

"The media fans the fire for ratings and the government, particularly the Republican-controlled Congress, fiddles while Washington burns!" Mitchell said. "The most powerful nation in the world is on a panty hunt and its leader is the target of a new Un-American Affairs Committee while the nation's and the world's pressing problems are ignored. It's a travesty!"

According to its creators, the "I Had Sex With Clinton, Too!" petition intends to do more than mock the Starr Report and send a message to Congress. "It's also a rallying cry for the millions of Americans who are outraged by what's happening," Weinstock stated. "The petition is on-going...until this national travesty is over. Unless we send a message to the Republican-controlled Congress that cannot be ignored—that they must stop the insanity of this partisan-inspired impeachment process—we will be sorrier for it as a nation and as individuals. We invite everyone to join our petition and 'confess'. The more confessions, the greater the impact. Take a stand! Or rather...jump in bed...and be counted."

Since its launch, the "I Had Sex With Clinton, Too!" website has logged over one million hits. Currently, visitors can read 12 confessions which are a "representative sample" of the more than 500 received to date. Provocative titles include: "Going All the Way! Under the Beltway! For the USA!", "I Met Bill Clinton In An AOL Chatroom & He Cybered Me Silly!", "The SeX-FILES", "Subpenis Envy" and "Deep Throat."

In 1998, during the hysteria of the Clinton sex scandal, hundreds of patriotic citizens demonstrated their support for President Clinton and protested the Independent Counsel's investigation by creating the most unusual petition in American history. They confessed to having sex with the President.

The "I Had Sex With Clinton, Too!" petition is a historic document, a rare example of democracy in action, and unlike any petition you learned about in school. It was created by nearly a thousand patriotic Americans who were outraged by the political and sexual hypocrisy of the Independent Counsel's investigation of President Bill Clinton. From all over the country, nearly a thousand citizens joined this cyber-protest march on Washington by confessing to their own imaginary sexual affair with Bill Clinton.

Like it or not, Donald Trump and the Republicans will be revisiting the Clinton sex scandals during this presidential election and beyond. To help us learn the lessons of the past, I'm making a sampling of the *"I Had Sex With Clinton, Too!"* petition available again as a prophylactic against sexually-transmitted STDs—*Scandal-induced Thought Distortions*. Through satire, the petition will inoculate us against being sex- scandaled once more, so Trump and the Republicans can't screw us again.

To the President and the First Lady...
for whom we have the utmost respect,

On behalf of our contributors, who've demonstrated their support for the President and the country in this most unusual, shocking and controversial way, we offer our apologies.

We hope you will view this protest in the satirical and supportive context it was meant. Sometimes we have to fight fire with fire! Fight hypocrisy with fantasy!

Jerry Weinstock & Joy Mitchell
Los Angeles, 1998

July 4, 1998
Office of the Independent Counsel,
Washington, D.C.

Dear Special Prosecutor, Kenneth Starr:

We have in our possession important information relevant to your investigation of President Clinton. Despite the shocking nature of this information, we realize it's our duty to come forward at this time for the good of the nation.

What follows is but a sample of the hundreds of confessions we've received from patriotic Americans who have "gotten into bed" with the President. These confessions describe in intimate and often graphic detail the sexual affairs and illicit encounters hundreds of people have had with President Clinton. It seems, Mr. Starr, your investigation has barely scratched the surface.

We must warn you, however, that these confessions are quite graphic in nature and so may be arousing, and therefore shocking, especially to someone like yourself!

Despite this, we urge you for the sake of the country to avail yourself of this valuable information, for we believe it sheds important new light on your investigation. We urge you to study these confessions carefully (this is only a sample and we will be happy to make them all available to you upon request).

We fervently believe these confessions constitute a unique petition in American history, and make it absolutely clear how most Americans feel.

Hoping you take this new information into your deliberations and that it motivates you to do the right thing—to act in the best interests of the country—and drop your investigation, we remain,

Sincerely,

Jerry Weinstock & Joy Mitchell

IT'S THE SEX, STUPID!

The Confessions

1. *"America the Bawdiful"*
2. *"A Harbor Tryst"*
3. *"Going All the Way!...Under the Beltway!...
   For the USA!"*
4. *"A Love Letter to Ken Starr"*
5. *"The SeX-FILES"*
6. *"A Muppet Confession"*
7. *"I Met Bill Clinton in an AOL Chatroom
   & He Cybered Me Silly!"*
8. *"Peach Pie"*
9. *"Bonking Billy"*
10. *"I Had Sex With Clinton...And His Little Dog, Too!"*
11. *"My Sexy Punishment from President Clinton"*
12. *"Snake Dance"*
13. *"MyFillofBill"*
14. *"The Jam Session"*
15. *"Deep Throat"*
16. *"I Feel So Cheap and Dirty..."*
17. *"Love at First Sound Bite"*
18. *"Starr's In My Eyes..."*
19. *"In Case You Want to Subpenis Me"*
20. *"Making an Ass of Myself"*

IT'S THE SEX, STUPID!

"America the Bawdiful"

Oh, beautiful for specious lies, for absent waves of brain,

For purple member majesties, inside a fruitful plane,

The President, The President,

He shed his grace on me,

And screwed me good like boyfriends should,

From sea to shining sea.

*— **Cindy B.**, Texas*

A Harbor Tryst

I am a National Parks Department employee. I will call myself simply "Libby" because I don't want my true identity revealed. I have been violated by Bill Clinton and this is my story.

I immigrated to this country many years ago from France and landed this wonderful job near Battery Park in New York City my very first day here. I have been a faithful and tireless civil servant and I've never missed a single day of work. It was on one such day at work that I first met Bill.

I will never forget that day. I saw him approaching me from a distance and, while to be truthful, I didn't know who he was at the time, I did recognize that look he had in his eyes.

I hope I don't sound too immodest by saying this, but I am used to being complimented all the time, by men and women alike. I could read the words on his lips as he approached.

"She's beautiful. The most beautiful lady I've ever seen."

Like I said, I've heard these sorts of compliments before, but there was something special about this particular man.

He had an air of confidence and power about him. While I'm not one to exhibit my emotions outwardly, he nearly made me drop my torch.

When his vehicle parked and he got out, I noticed that he was accompanied by several Secret Service agents as well as two women, one who I later discovered to be his wife and the other his daughter. Despite this entourage watching his every move, Bill fixed his gaze on my eyes and didn't break it as he approached me. Most men will look away, but not Bill. Like I said, it was that obvious confidence that got to me.

Bill walked right up to me and soon, without saying a word, he worked his way under my long flowing robe. Another moment and he was inside of me.

I'm not ashamed to admit it, I was glad he was there. I'm also not ashamed to admit that he stayed inside of me for over an hour, exploring all that I had to offer. And it made me feel so good! I hadn't felt that good in years, not even when that other President visited me for my birthday.

When Ronnie was here, there were fireworks for sure. But Ronnie was faking it, he never even went inside. But not Bill! Bill was the real thing. Ronnie just wanted to be seen with me, but Bill didn't care if he was seen with me or not; he just wanted to be part of me.

When Bill finally exited, I could tell that he was as satisfied as I was. As he and his entourage walked away, he looked back at me, over his shoulder. And, though I'm not positive because the glare of the sun made it difficult to see, I thought I read the words I longed for on his lips, 'I love you, "Libby"'.

That was the last time I saw him in person.

I'm not writing this letter to hurt Bill or for any personal gain. It's just that with all that's been said and written about him recently, I just wanted him to know that I still remember that one day he came to visit me. And even though I've had many other visitors since, I'll always treasure our terse but torrid tryst by the harbor.

"Libby"

Going All The Way!
...Under The Beltway!
...For The Good Old USA!

A friend of mine and I had decided
That were the funds and time provided
that we would have to be derided
Were we not to be invited

To the Nation's Capitol, one fine spring day
On Spring vacation, that month of May
To see the sights, and run and play
My friend made plans, I said "Hooray!"

So on the bus we piled our stuff,
(To pack it up was kind of tough,
You hear 'bout the Capitol being rough
So you don't want to take any guff...)

But I brought my own black satin gown,
The skirt of it was circled round
With bugle beads and finer things,
I brought diamond earrings and some gold rings...

IT'S THE SEX, STUPID!

So anyway, once we hit town,
Unpacked our bags and looked around,
Checked into our hotel, it was downtown,
On TV we heard a special sound

Selections would be held that very day
By the President of the USA
A cattle call, guess you could say
We were late! to our dismay!!

We arrived at the White House after running
Into the bathroom so we'd look stunning
My friend hadn't brought a dress that she could wear
So she used Coke cans to set her hair

We made a dress in nothing flat
(the problem is, my friend's, um, fat)
So we wrapped her round in sheets of white
Making sure to pin it right
It looked kind of cool, I had to say
To see her all dressed up that way

See, the thing is you must look stunning
If you want to be in the running...
One must be sharp, one must be sly,
When trying to attract that special guy...

When we arrived, disaster struck!
The women were climbing off a truck

Buses! Cars! Whole planeloads, too!
My friend said, "See!! I told you!"

The problem is the call had gone
on TV, where it was run
In fifteen time-zones, Satellite too
From Zambia to Kalamazoo...

Women came running when they got the chance
to make Clinton do the trouser dance
Women of every size, from every nation!
Every age and race, and orientation

I looked behind me, saw my friend Katie,
My high school principal, and her cleaning lady...
The Queen of England! Diana Ross!
Nastassia Kinski, and Kate Moss.

More humanity than I had seen
Piling onto the White House green
Pretty soon the lawn filled up
So they sent policemen to round us up

Made everyone all get in line
Gave us numbers, (something fine)
Assigned us numbers, took our picture
Searched our purses, gave us liquor

I stood all night and through next day
Because I knew I had one sure way

IT'S THE SEX, STUPID!

to have my turn with Willie C
And see if he was the man for me

All around me women waited
And did their nails, wond'ring how Clinton rated
Every now and then a girl'd come blushing
Attended by a number of rushing
Folks trailing behind her, wanting to know
Had she gotten in? Where did she go??

But it was easy, plain to see
The girls who had climbed the banana tree
Each one was smiling from ear to ear
And I started to feel a sinking fear

What if Clinton wore out before he got to me?
What would I tell people, where would I be?
Now that I was there my heart was set on
Sex with Clinton, more than I let on

The line moved slowly, till there I was
Going through the black gates and cause
I had some such a long way and looked so cute
The guards rushed me to the front of the route

They ran me through an underground trail
Through twists and turns, until I failed
to know up from down, or left from right,
but then I popped out to a delightful sight:

Don't Let TRUMP & the GOP Sex-Scandal US Again!

The President of the USA!
and don't you know I'd have to say
The way he looked, while there he lay
Was the finest thing I've seen to this day!

He wore gold pajamas, with a sash
Smoking a cigar from a large brown cache
Lying back in bed, on satin sheets
Looking slightly tired, but not that beat
He looked like he could take MY heat

I tore off my veil and jumped in bed!
(I jumped so high I hit my head...)
The Secret Service shut the door,
And told me they would say no more

In bed with Clinton I frolicked there,
He kissed me tenderly, and touched my hair
He touched me high, and touched me low
Till I was insane, and knew where to go
He drove me wild with sexy ways
The best lover I've had unto this day

I learned something after that day
With the President of the USA
It doesn't matter what they say
About these things from day to day...

The thing that's sad, I'd have to say
Is that people are allowing Ken Starr today

IT'S THE SEX, STUPID!

To waste more money than seems quite right
Following facts that don't come to light

Based on a story like I've told you
About as honest, and about as true
It seems to me there are people who
Don't really have much else to do

Poor lil Monica had no sense
And now pays millions for her defense
Because Ken Starr is sitting pretty
In charge of the NEW Un-American Affairs Committee.

Let us all join hands and pray
That very soon we'll see the day
When Americans snap into their thoughts
Get rid of Ken Starr and the whole lot.

The fact that this all drags on don't seem right
While times are hard and money's tight,
Let the President do his work.
I have just one thought—Ken Starr's a jerk.

— A Former Clinton White House Staffer

A Love Letter To Ken Starr

An Open Love Letter To Kenneth Starr
Independent Counsel
Investigating The Sex Life Of President Clinton

My Precious and Most Esteemed Mr. Starr,

You don't know me, but I'm a secret admirer of you. I think you are the sexiest man in the world. Since you started probing into the sex lives of President Bill Clinton and Monica Lewinsky, I've wanted to marry you.

If I wasn't a man, I'd want to have your baby. You make me want to wear lingerie, and leather bondage goods. All for you, my man of torture!

I started having all of these hot and nasty feelings for you when you started investigating the sex life of Bill Clinton.

I've been so hot since then, Kenny (can I call you Kenny?) I haven't been able to go to sleep each night until I kiss your picture I cut out of *Time* magazine.

IT'S THE SEX, STUPID!

I have your tyrannical image on the wall in my bedroom next to Hitler, Stalin and Jeffrey Dahmer. The thought of you probing into Billy's sex life really turns me on, I mean in a big way, big boy.

Kenny, dear (can I call you dear?) I know what you want, and I want to give it to you. Will you please do me a real hot favor? Subpoena me to the grand jury. I've been intimate with Senator Jesse Helms, half the pages in congress, a couple of federal judges, and Janet Reno.

When I was with Jesse Helms, he got real excited when I talked about queers, atheists and communists. But it's you, dear Kenny. You're the one I want.

If you're looking to interrogate someone about sex, please, Kenny, pick me! I can tell you about how Bob Dornan couldn't get it up for a Mexican democrat. But he just about died of ecstasy when I set him up with a transsexual abortion rights activist.

While you're at it, will you please subpoena my mother to the grand jury? Grill her about my sex life. Drill her with your penetrating presence. The more you humiliate her, the more you rule over me, Sir.

And if that doesn't get both of us going, sweety, then I have another hot idea in my nasty bag of tricks. Will you role-play for me, my dear tyrant? I want you to be Senator Joseph McCarthy. You know, the guy you have replaced in history. That's why I love you so much. You remind me of his paranoid, totalitarian ways.

Please, Kenny baby! I want to hear you ask me, like you really mean it: "Are you now, or have you ever been a member of the Communist party?"

Then, if you want me over and over again, you can subpoena my friends to testify against me. Nothing gets me more hot than knowing my friends have turned against me. Kenny, my dominator! Degrade me! Call me bad names! Make the press hate me! You brute! I want to lick your boots. (You do wear big, black boots, don't you?)

But you know what really gets my juices flowing? The fact that you've spent $40 million going after Billy Clinton. Talk about potency, Kenny! You really know how to keep it up! You can really blow a wad! If you reach $100 million, my tyrant, I'll marry you, my stallion, my stud!

But, let me tell you a secret, darling. When I think how much you'll spend to expose the sex life of one man, I get really wet when I think anybody else could be next. If we just opened up everybody's bedroom, think of the fun you and I could have together.

I'm dying to know what goes on in YOUR private life, my dear. By the way, do you like to cuddle? Do you use whips and chains? Master! Throw away the constitution and tie me down! My love, I would give my right nut to be on the grand jury! To hear all those nasty little secrets would make me love you forever. My cute little dictator!

IT'S THE SEX, STUPID!

But, please tell me dear. Do the jurors have private peeping booths from which to view the proceedings? And do those booths have tissue boxes to clean up with afterwards? You know, they must really get hot after hearing all that nasty sex talk. I go wild just hearing about it on the news.

I know you're just dying to know all about Billy's little willy. You must have an awesome crush on him. You little devil.

I used to think I wanted to be a Pentecostal preacher, cause I could get all the fried chicken and bush I could eat. But, you've inspired me to change my mind. Now I'm going to law school so I can be an inquisitor. But tell me. Do they still use anal probes like they did in the middle ages?

You make me proud to be an American. You, my good sir, have the sexiest job in the whole country. How I envy you.

If you really want to get off, my dear, read the Malleus Maleficarum, Foxe's Book of Martyrs, and The Salem Witch Trials. I'm sure you must have one of the manuals of torture, published by the U.S. Government for the School of the Americas, at Fort Benning, Georgia, otherwise known as the School of Assassins, the U.S. training camp of right wing Latin American dictators.

The manual, Interrogation and Combat Intelligence, makes my panties wet. And, no doubt, you have read Justine by de Sade and Venus of Furs, by Sacher-Masoch. You must know all the secrets of sado-masochism.

You are the nastiest man on the planet. If I told you I had sex with the devil, I'll bet that would make you love me. You sweet brute!

If you're looking for somebody to bust for lying, I can do it real good. Just humiliate me with your interrogations and I'll lie down anywhere you say. Since I found my true love in you, my dear, the word "deposition" is my favorite little jingle which tingles my dingle.

I want you to question me with everything you have, baby. I'll take it all in, the whole rule of law. I want you to give me all the inquisition you've got. I'll be your slave. I'll lie for you. I'll give up all my rights and allow you to degrade me. I'll swallow every drop of your interrogation, Master.

Please, Kenny, give it to me in a big way! Maybe together, we can really get this country going in the right direction.

Submissively awaiting your reply,

Mercury Coyote

The SeX-*FILES*

Dear Special Prosecutor:

I have intimate knowledge of the subject you are investigating. And though you say you only want the truth, I don't think you can handle the truth, the unbelievable Truth.

I am a woman. I am an intelligence officer. My identity must remain concealed. I am disobeying orders by revealing this information to you. But as you will see, I have no choice.

Mr. Starr, isn't it ironic that your moral crusade—which you refer to as your investigation—has forced so many good and decent and patriotic Americans to break their most cherished vows and bonds.

Well, here's the truth Mr. Starr—can you handle it?!

There is something called the Blue Book project that deals with our government's secret contacts with UFO's and Extra-terrestrials, ETs.

After President Clinton's inauguration in '92, he was debriefed as to how to contact the extra-terrestrial visitors who have been here since the dawn of history.

The President wondered about their intentions. He was assured that this star-faring, inter-galactic civilization, like the Federation on Star Trek, practiced non-intervention as their Prime Directive, albeit with one qualification—they make themselves available to the Leader of the World they are visiting who can contact them and ask for advice.

Immediately following his debriefing, which was eye-opening to say the least, President Clinton, accompanied by some handpicked women from the various intelligence agencies, was taken aboard an alien spacecraft—a UFO, a starship—and as President of the United States, Leader of the most powerful nation on Earth, William Jefferson Clinton was introduced to the ET delegation and offered the benefit of their wisdom.

Most importantly, he was shown how to contact them whenever he wished their counsel.

He was informed that this wasn't the first time they've established contact with human leaders. Throughout history they've maintained a relationship with leaders throughout the world.

"How?" Bill wanted to know.

Bill was expecting to be given some hand-held device like a cell phone or a tricorder. But when the ETs realized what he had in mind, they laughed at our primitiveness. And yes, they are very much like us, and they do laugh. A lot.

IT'S THE SEX, STUPID!

So they explained to him that truly advanced civilizations don't communicate with machines, but rather tune their own spirit-body, their own bio-organic transmitter to the proper dimensional channel…and presto! Nothing gets lost in the translation. There is no translation! There's only direct communication from one mind directly to the other.

And so the President was shown how he could contact these "Friends" whenever he wanted and receive their counsel about any issue that concerned the welfare of the people of the world.

The President was very excited about this opportunity. There were so many problems. Being President was so complicated. A lot tougher than being a Governor. This would help him gain perspective, gain wisdom… He couldn't wait.

And so he and his aides were trained… And sworn to secrecy.

How do I know this? I was one of those aides.

Since 1993, whenever President Clinton needed advice on critical matters he would call in a "secretary" (that's what we were called.)

And she…we…would "tune" him, as we'd been taught by the ETs, so that he could communicate telepathically with the ET Council.

Now this is the hard one for all of us earthlings to handle. You see, this "tuning" would look to an outside observer like a "blow job."

According to the ETs, cock-sucking, when done in a very particular way, can put one in touch with them.

Now it was imperative that the President not orgasm so that he wouldn't lose the telepathic connection with the ET Council, so we were shown various techniques to prevent that.

Most importantly we were taught the "song" we had to "sing," actually hum, while we sucked the President's cock. And it was the sucking and singing and some other secret things which we did that "tuned" him.

This "song" is composed of a series of sounds or notes…a very rudimentary melody. But it should come as no surprise if you've seen the movie, Close Encounters. ETs are partial to music as a means of communication.

For lack of a better word the melody became known as the "Secretary's Song." And here's how it went.

First, we would stimulate the President's penis until he had an erection. After all the training I'd undergone, I didn't think of it as sex at all, but rather I felt like a NASA technician at mission control. Really! And his growing erection seemed to me like a bio-organic antenna being deployed.

We have full deployment, Houston!

Seriously, though, we took our jobs very seriously. And so did the President.

IT'S THE SEX, STUPID!

The President had been instructed by the ETs how to perform secret visualizations, breathing and other top secret techniques which I gathered worked like a beacon to "tune" the President's electromagnetic body, his energy field.

I would sing the Secretary's Song with his erect penis in my mouth, and like a tuning fork the sound would travel from the antenna of his penis into his body and then into the energy body that connects to that place where there is no space and time.

The way it was explained to me, the Song would shift his vibratory rate and that would subtly shift his dimensional matrix and, Voila, the beacon he'd been visualizing would become activated. And if we did everything the way we were supposed to, the President would be in telepathic contact with the ET Council. And without him having to even think his question, they'd answer him.

Mission accomplished.

My job was to deploy his "antenna" and "tune" him to shift his dimensional matrix so he could obtain contact with the ETs and then make sure he didn't orgasm and lose contact. It was a job I took very seriously. Often the fate of the world hung in the balance.

Many is the time a crisis had developed and I was the "secretary" called into the Oval Office to "tune" the President so he could contact the ET Council.

At first, I was inexperienced. Oh I'd given my fair share of blow jobs, in fact, I considered myself a cock-sucking artist…but that was my problem. There was still a part of me that wanted to get him off…make him come…see him climax.

People think that sucking cock is demeaning. I've always experienced a tremendous power over any man whose cock I had in my mouth. And somehow all those old ways of thinking, old habits, crept in and sure enough the President would orgasm and lose contact.

It took a lot of discipline on my part and eventually, I am proud to say, once the President was deployed and inserted in my mouth and I sang the Song, I could guarantee his telepathic contact with the ETs for as long as he wanted. In fact, I became so good at my job, I flatter myself into thinking I was his favorite Secretary.

I've served several Presidents as Secretary. Some employed our services more than others. All had difficulty coming to terms with it—couldn't see past the "blow job," "cock-sucking" mindset.

I remember that during our training on the alien spacecraft, we were introduced to our trainers who were both male and female. "These are some of our greatest Singers," the ETs told us.

What they were actually saying was, "These men and women are some of our most honored and prized cock-suckers!" Talk about culture shock! I've never thought about cock-sucking in the same way since.

IT'S THE SEX, STUPID!

In fact, I couldn't have done what I did, serving the President and our country in the way I did without shedding many of my beliefs about sex. In fact, that was the first thing we were told by the ETs…that our emotional and mental attitudes particularly about sex would have a great impact on the success or failure of the mission. They said that our attitudes about sex were the keys to our evolution. That blew my mind.

Of all the Presidents I've served, President Clinton had the least difficulty coming to terms with this very new and different way of thinking. I tend to think it's because Bill Clinton is a child of the 60's, and though he claims he didn't inhale, he absorbed by osmosis the sexual and cultural revolution that was going on.

And because President Clinton was the most comfortable with these "alien" concepts, he availed himself of the ET's counsel and their wisdom more than any other President.

Over time I came to admire his courage and stamina. There was always a risk of exposure. Of misunderstanding. Of scandal. But President Clinton wanted to serve the nation in the best way possible. And so gain invaluable advice concerning the many great difficulties we face, not only as a nation but as a world community and a planet.

And so he used our services fairly regularly.

There were several of us, as you can imagine. We moved with him wherever he went like the black box or red telephone that is never far away. We were always on call.

Sometimes we were even disguised as men. But we were always there, like the Secret Service, always ready to serve.

Reading over this confession, I see that many of your readers are going to think I'm making salacious puns when I say, "serve our Leader". But that's not my intent. There's no other way to express how I felt.

I know I speak for the others, when I say—It was the greatest honor to get down on our knees, deploy the President's penis and sing him into contact with the ET Council.

It was my greatest honor to serve the President, the country and the world in this way! And from way up there in space inside the ET starship looking down on the blue jewel that is the Earth, you see that it's just one world and we're all in it together.

We've all taken vows of silence. But I feel so strongly about the "scandal" and the terrible damage it's doing, especially to our relations with the ETs, that I'm violating my oath, possibly on pain of death, to plead the President's case.

You see, he's also sworn to silence by the ETs. And he's between a rock and a hard place. Were he to break the intergalactic agreement—being sworn to secrecy—the ETs would break off relations with the planet, and no future President would have the benefit of their advice and counsel. That would be the greatest tragedy imaginable for humanity.

So President Clinton will keep silent…while the media jokes about the "Presidential knee pads." And who knows?

I certainly don't know who all the "secretaries" are… Maybe Monica is one, too!

And so, Mr. Starr, I think this investigation into the President's sex life is the greatest threat not only to national security but to world peace. If we lose contact with the ETs, who have been guiding our civilization for thousands of years, we will be putting ourselves in grave danger. So for the love of God, give the President a break, let him have his private moments. You have no idea what's at stake!

Yours forever in service

with a song on my lips,

and the President's antenna in my mouth,

A Patriotic American

A Muppet Confession

Dear Special Prosecutor:

I wish I could tell you who I am—because then you'd be even more shocked that a sow of my stature has been asked to muddy herself publicly by telling-all about our President. But I must protect My Frog Charming.

My tail loses its curl over the very idea of having sex with the President. I mean, what's a pig of my caste doing with someone who feeds from the public trough? Alas, I saw that little pudgy face of Billy's, that snout resembling so many in my family photo album, that porky belly he used to have—well...

As you may know, I hire someone to exercise for me—I just can't be bothered. My Hired Exerciser confided to me that Billy used to have a Hired Exerciser, a man who works for the same outfit. I asked if perhaps my exerciser could arrange for me to meet the President. Just to pinch his little cheeks—nothing more, I assure you.

About three years ago, Hillary Clinton called me. She was oh-so-polite but soon let go of her important-lady voice.

She practically gushed. Said she'd always wanted to meet me, likes what I stand for, and so on. She wasn't Billy, but what the heck.

Ms. Clinton met me at Porky's, a fine dining establishment just outside of Graceland. She told our waitress that she was very, very hungry and ordered four hot dogs and some fries. But she ate only a potato chip and sipped sarsaparilla. Then she asked for a doggie bag into which she slipped the dogs and fries. I bet Socks and Whatzisname never saw those wieners.

Ms. Clinton looked absolutely gorgeous in hot pink Spandex tights, a hot-pink and yellow polka-dot athletic bra, and white platform tennies. Her dark glasses had gyrating, glittery miniature Elvises jutting out from each side. Tiny, teeny stereo speakers hung from her earrings. She had the volume turned down so I didn't catch what she was playing, but that woman can sure move her curves, I'm telling you!

What did I think of her outfit? I thought it was too, too, too cute. She agreed to order me a complete set, from Barbra Streisand I believe she said. I bet if she dressed like that more often, these rumors about Billy and other women would cease.

The First Lady confessed her abiding crush for my frog, which really made my hairs stand on end. But her snout is no match for mine, her corpulence not nearly as pink-perfect as mine. I agreed to convey her affectionate salutation to my true love. Then remembering I had to get to a hair appointment, I pressed her to tell me why she'd called for this little tete-a-tete.

"Why to meet you in real life. To find out more than I can read in the magazines," but her little smile began to bend, fold and mutilate.

"And why is that?" I have only so much patience for groupies.

"Well, Ms. —," and she said my name, "may I call you P—?"

"No."

"Oh, well, Ms. —, my husband has been talking in his sleep for years about you. He says the most... the most... well, I've long ago learned to keep my lips zipped, especially on bedroom subjects. Your exerciser gave us your cell-phone number and here I am."

Hillary interviewed me basically. I had an O.K. time hamming it up. Then she said she'd like to have her husband meet me. My little heart went pitapat and I had to pause for a good fanning. A strange thing happened toward the end of our time together; that's when I lent the tearful lady my hanky.

You see, Ms. Clinton confessed, "I used to fix Bill up with lots of women when he was, you know, obscene—oh dear, I mean, porcine. But now that he's slimmed down, I really want to keep him for myself. Maybe if I gift him with an evening in your presence, he'll be more eager to please me."

She stopped sniffling and her voice was strong as pigs' knuckles. "By the way, I've been meaning to contribute to your fine work with Restore the Barnyards."

Talk about pork barrels!

IT'S THE SEX, STUPID!

Later that year, I met the President alone in their bedroom at the White House. The walls were lined with pictures. Pictures of Chelsea as a little girl. Chelsea in the Hoover Tower at Stanford (lovingly known as Hoover's Last Erection). Hillary graduating from law school. John Kennedy shaking Billy's hand. Billy's Mamma. Not one girlie picture except mine, over the place the President tucks his jammies under the pillow at the White House. Isn't that too, too cute?

Billy—he asked me to call him Bill but I told him it was Billy or nothing—asked me to make myself comfortable. I swooshed my boa at him—I'm entitled to one teensy flirt—and spread myself across the chenille spread on the only piece of furniture in the room.

The President walked to the window and spoke with his back to me. And here is what he said.

"Ms. P., I have adored you since I saw your first movie. The flounce of your hair, the way you dress, the roundness of you. Like Jack Kennedy, I have lusted—but like Jimmy, only in my heart—after screen actresses. I been dreamin' of us together watchin' videos, lickin' ice cream cones... so many delicious poses I see us in. I wonder... "

The President's voice faded. He turned toward me, backed up with a start when he saw that I had raised my skirt just a tad, blushed and turned away again.

"I wonder," he said, "if you could go to the press and declare that we have made mad passionate love with one another." And his voice lifted the way Southerners do when they're trying to make a statement but it comes out sounding like a question.

"You see the other women I asked to do this have botched the whole thing. I would never have sex with anyone but myself. However, I need," and here his voice sounded like one of those southern preachers, "neeedddd to have a female followin'— the Party's gotta have the female voters—passionate but intelligent women. The world knows you have a mind that won't quit. Could you go to the press, make up a story that I am equipped to outshine any porker? That my tongue knows no bounds? That my hands slipped over your sides like a man handling diamonds? Would you, please?"

Dear World, I have too much integrity for such big lies. I never had sex with the President. And I doubt he had sex with any of the other women he asked to tell those big fibs. I totally, totally, totally love the man's leadership prowess. But for a sex object, I'll take my frog any day.

Miss Anonymous

I Met Bill Clinton in an AOL Chatroom & He Cybered Me Silly!

I first met Bill in a "Married But Flirty" chatroom on America OnLine. His screen name was BIGBILL4U, and he was funny and charming in the chatroom.

I didn't realize he was President until much later when he complained that his wife didn't understand him because she got too many ideas about feminism from Oprah and from watching old newsreels of Eleanor Roosevelt.

And she hated "oral sex," he said.

I wondered how she got her hands on the old newsreels and it dawned on me she must have some executive access.

When he said he was from Arkansas but "stationed in Washington DC," I put 2 and 2 together.

Luckily, Bill seemed to like me and began to Instant Message me. I saved some of the IM conversations.

This was our first:

BIGBILL4U: hi sweets

Picnic 6:   hi BB4U, how are you?

BIGBILL4U: I'm better now that I met you,
                  Sugar Dumplin'

Picnic 6:   Oh, really? :) Why's that?

BIGBILL4U: Well, darlin' I just have a hunch you have
                  a real way with men.

Picnic 6:   a hunch, huh?

BIGBILL4U: I love a good hunch, don't you?

Picnic 6:   You mean a hump? Is hunching like
                  humping where you come from?

BIGBILL4U: It's exactly like that Baby--you catch
                  on quick.

Picnic 6:   So tell me about yourself, Big

BIGBILL4U: I am big...lol

Picnic 6:   hahahahah... how big?

BIGBILL4U: Big enough to tickle your pretty little
                  tonsils, baby

Picnic 6:   Wow! You don't beat around the bush
                  do you?

BIGBILL4U:	LOL some say I beat Bush pretty darn good a few years back!
Picnic 6:	huh?
BIGBILL4U:	nevermind...brb, I spilled some donut sugar on my keyboard
Picnic 6:	you eat while you are chatting?
BIGBILL4U:	Baby I can eat while I'm "having a hunch" LOL ;)
Picnic 6:	gross!
BIGBILL4U:	Don't knock it till you try it Baby Doll!
Picnic 6:	hmmm
BIGBILL4U:	Will you be here later? I gotta go to some damn meeting
Picnic 6:	Yes! Meet you later?
BIGBILL4U:	After the late news?
Picnic 6:	Sure.
BIGBILL4U:	See you then, Sugar Babe.
Picnic 6:	***
BIGBILL4U:	(Picnic)***
Picnic 6:	Bye, Big Boy!

Later that night:

BIGBILL4U: Hey Babe

Picnic 6:   hmmm, you came back!

BIGBILL4U: 'Course I did, little Bill has been awake since I IMMED you earlier

Picnic 6:   little Bill?

BIGBILL4U: yeah, he lives in my pants! LOL ;)

Picnic 6:   Oh, you!

BIGBILL4U: So what do you have on, Baby Doll?

Picnic 6:   A T-shirt and panties, and you?

BIGBILL4U: Ummmm sounds good, I have on a suit still.

Picnic 6:   at this hour?

BIGBILL4U: well shall I take it off-or just unzip the pants?

Picnic 6:   hmmm

BIGBILL4U: I want you to meet the Boss!

Picnic 6:   Is that Little Bill?

BIGBILL4U: Yep! But he's not THAT little!

Picnic 6:   How little is he?

BIGBILL4U: after meeting you, he is HUGE

Picnic 6:   and what does he want?

BIGBILL4U: a kiss

Picnic 6:   from me?

BIGBILL4U: Only You, Sugar Baby

Picnic 6:   How do you think I can accomplish
                that online?

BIGBILL4U: Describe it to me baby

Picnic 6:   well, I would, uhhh, but...

BIGBILL4U: come on Baby

Picnic 6:   well, what do you want me to do?

BIGBILL4U: I like a big wet sloppy French kiss

Picnic 6:   On Little Bill?

BIGBILL4U: Yep! But he's not THAT little!
                He's HUGE right now, Baby!

P. S. Here's a bit more from my IM chats with "You Know Who:"

BIGBILL4U: hi baby doll, how you doing?

Picnic 6:   hi Big Boy, I'm fine, but I still have
                a sore cyber throat

BIGBILL4U: how come, darlin'?

Picnic 6:   Well, you were pretty rough on me last night

BIGBILL4U: Sorry babe, it's just that you bring out
                the stallion in me

Picnic 6:   That explains all that twitching
                and whinnying

BIGBILL4U: So, what have you got for me today, sugar?

Picnic 6:   Well... have you ever mixed food and sex
                at the same time?

BIGBILL4U: Oh BABY! Little Bill is perking up fast!
                What did you have in mind?

Picnic 6:   Do you like banana cream pie?

BIGBILL4U: Oh Gawd! Do I ever! (So does Little
                Hard Bill!)

Picnic 6:   How'd you like me to smash a pie all over
                little Bill and his buddies?

BIGBILL4U: Then would you lick it off?

Picnic 6:   :)

BIGBILL4U: We may have to meet. Can you keep
                a secret?

Picnic 6:   huh?

BIGBILL4U: Well, I have a kinda big shot job here in DC.

Picnic 6:   oh?

BIGBILL4U: Yeah, and it's one of those security
              clearance type jobs

Picnic 6:   So I would have to be discrete- is that what
              you are saying?

BIGBILL4U: Oh Baby, you ARE quick on the uptake.
              Yes you would.Very much so.

Picnic 6:   hmmm...can you call me and tell me
              all about it?

BIGBILL4U: Only if you describe for me in detail
              about that banana cream pie, Baby

Picnic 6:   You got it, stallion

BIGBILL4U: I have your phone number already, I had
              some assistants get it for me...

Picnic 6:   How did you manage that, Mister Man?

BIGBILL4U: My lips are sealed, Baby : X Hey lemme
              call you now, hon.

Picnic 6:   I'll log off now and wait by the phone,
                 horsey boy.

BIGBILL4U: You get that pie ready, darlin'.
                 Call you in 5 minutes. ***

                      Dear Special Prosecutor

                      Hope this whets your appetite a bit,

                                        Picnic

Peach Pie

Dear Mr. Special Prosecutor:

I have a confession to make that most certainly will rock your whole investigation. I cannot contain my story anymore, as I have my eye on one of those cute new Volkswagen Beetles and I feel confident that someone from the tabloid media will certainly pay me enough to purchase one.

I, too, have had the pleasure of making love to William J. Clinton. It was early 1996, and I was pulling a double at the truck stop where I work.

One of my regulars, Leon Briggs, had lost his dog behind the restaurant again, and I was out there whistling for him (I'm the loudest whistler in three counties, so I was the natural choice to help find old Killer).

Anyways, Bill was out campaigning for re-election. My truck stop is right off I-79 in a little town in West Virginia. I guess Bill was on his way to Charleston when he saw our sign and realized he was hankering after some truck stop peach pie.

He heard me whistling before he saw me. And then when I came back inside, well, I guess he was pretty much impressed with the whole package.

He was such a gentleman. He leaned over the counter at me and winked. "Darlin," he said, "I'd just love to wet that whistle."

Now, I'm a waitress. I hear that line at least once a day, and most of the men that say that to me are nothing more than redneck pigs. But when our President Clinton said it to me, it about melted my heart. I finished giving fresh coffee to all of my tables and had a few quiet minutes to myself. I had been planning to run back to the kitchen, smoke a Lucky Strike and check the lottery numbers in the paper, but in that instant, well, my plans changed.

The President and I hustled our butts back to the employee restroom. His manly body crashed into me in a wave of passion.

"I don't know what it is about waitress uniforms," he said, "but I get horny every time I see one."

I moaned with anticipation. My lips parted and I arched my back just like they do on the covers of romance novels. This was a classy guy and I wanted him to know I was every bit his match.

I put a few strips of toilet paper on the floor and kneeled on them (any waitress knows that dirt from the bathroom floor'll show up on panty hose the way bird shit does to a clean car). Bill quickly unbuckled his belt and opened his pants. He leaned against the sink and faced me. His face was beginning to glisten with sweat and his breathing was all ragged. He lovingly clasped my head in his big hands and led me to his engorged manhood. I looked upon it with wonder for a moment, and then I began to pleasure the presidential penis.

I felt sure that I would swoon, for this was not just any old pecker. It was tall, proud and smelled like expensive cologne. My husband ain't never perfumed his package before, and I wonder if he had, if I would have stayed with him.

Anyways, I sucked on Bill with as much force as the muscles in my mouth and throat would allow.

After a time, Bill let forth a series of high giggly moans that sounded like "hee hee hee ohhhhh, ohhhhh, ohhhhhh, ohhhhh," his penis began to throb, and then he let forth a great wave of slick spunk.

I hung on until his orgasm subsided and then I backed away and looked up at his face. He was beaming at me with happiness and pride.

"Thank you," he said, "you have relieved a great burden from deep inside me. I have so many pressures every day, and" (he glanced at my name tag), "Chayleen, in these last few moments, you have skillfully removed those pressures and helped me to recall what it feels like to be a man. I am so grateful to you, and I consider you a fine asset to this great country. Here, let me help you up."

He hitched his hands under my armpits and stood me upright. He left the bathroom first, and then, after fixing my lipstick, I followed a minute later so as not to arouse any suspicions.

I entered the dining room carrying a whole peach pie that I had wrapped for the president to take with him. I handed it to him and whispered "Next time you come through here, stop long enough to taste a better pie than this one!" He smiled a winning smile, winked suggestively at me, and was out the door.

I re-play that magical afternoon in my head all the time. The president was warm, gentle, and so sexy. I wish you would stop making such a fuss over him. I, for one, think he is a great leader. I'd vote for him again and again.

Well, anyways, that's my story. I want a book deal and a blue Beetle. Please see what you can do.

Thank you very much.

Shelly M., aka Chayleen

Bonking Billy

One Night Real Late
I sought to mate
On the telephone line
At economy rate

So I dialed and dialed on the double ohh Eight
And I got slick Willie as he trolled his bait.
Well Hi lill Darhlin my little Ozzie mate
How'd you like come to grips with this ol head of state

Is That You MR. President
Yeh babe, it's true.
An mah shlongs so big it's gone from red to blue.
So sweet baby please keep talkin dirty do
Be a hound dog,
Give mah bone a damm good chew

So I got a puffin and a pantin
And the monkey got a spankin
And I played Bill's horn until it finally blew

Don't Let TRUMP & the GOP Sex-Scandal US Again!

I'm not going to tell the rest
At my publishers behest
Cause there's cash in bonking Billie
Sure bet it's true.

"No shit!" said Linda Tripp when Monica made her slip
"Sure thing," she said to Kath and Paula, too
If you want to make some bucks from your presidential fucks
Go see Kenneth Starr and he'll come through.

But unlike those other bitches
Who happily drop their britches
And then cry foul when all is said and done
I'm absolutely shameless
So your President is blameless
If I could vote he'd be my number one.

So from Australia I say Shame
To this sick and sorry game
You have a great man in Washington
Yes you do

It's a really lousy spin for the Right to try and win
By trying to play the man and not the game.

Deborah Wenham
Brisbane, Australia

P.S. To the sane people of America:
Your (web) page has restored my faith

I Had Sex With Clinton...
...And His Little Dog, Too!

As Air Force One touched down on the sizzling tarmac, the President, flushed and sweaty as Susan Carpenter MacMillan in the throes of a menopausal hotflash, drawled "Was it as good for you as it was for me?"

My name is Dodiebell Eugenia Fuchs and I, like countless other clean-living women of impeccable morality, was ravished by Bill Clinton... and his little dog, too! This is my story.

As an operative for the VRWC (Vast Right Wing Conspiracy), I was given my assignment by "Deep Scrote" (who has always sounded suspiciously like Pat Buchanan, but we Footsoldiers for Fidelity don't ask questions.) My job was to infiltrate the White House inner circle by any means necessary.

After numerous futile attempts to catch the President's eye, I underwent electrolysis (What can I say? I come from a long line of hirsute women) and breast augmentation. Suddenly, I was more popular than chitt'lins at an Arkansas barbecue and on the government payroll!

My job was to carry around the box that Stephanopolous stood on during photo ops. As a double agent, it was my responsibilty to root through the White House laundry and sniff the Presidential boxers for evidence of sexual wrongdoing. (Clinton's undies are readily identified by the "I'm with Stupid" slogan embroidered on the pouch).

One hot, summer day in '93...or maybe it was '94...might have been Spring...whatever...anyway, the President and entourage, which included myself and the box, were aboard Air Force One as it streaked its way toward California and a clambake with some of those negro feminazi LA politicians.

I had snuck into the Presidential bedroom to count prophylactics when the door flew open...

....and there stood the Commander in Chief. With a grin on his face and a salami in his pocket, he was all over me like gravy on roadkill!

His right hand digging into my Frederick's of Hollywood foam rubber "Enhance-a-Fanny", he used his left to hang a needlepoint plaque on the outside door..."If the plane is rockin', don't bother knockin.'"

Pressing himself against my breasts, he remarked "I've seen bowling balls with more give!" Ripping my bosoms from their encasements, he continued "And better nipples on a Playtex Nurser!"

IT'S THE SEX, STUPID!

But that didn't stop him. Oh noooo! Using Hillary's pantyhose, he trussed me up like a holiday turkey. (I suggested using something of a less delicate weave, but true to form, that selfish boor didn't care that we...I mean he...was destroying his wife's stockings!) Bill Clinton had me stripped, strapped and stroked faster than Newt Gingrich can say "Welfare Queen".

An hour or two into this orgy...err...I mean ordeal, during which I was rendered speechless, I felt something like a giant suction cup attached to my left leg. That mangey mutt Buddy was having his way with my calf!

(Buddy didn't come on to the scene until '97??? Ok, well... then this happened in '97...or it was another dog named Buddy...or maybe it was a cat...did the Clintons ever have a pet 'possum?...whatever....)

The final insult was the President's failure to send flowers the following day, nor even a note of thanks. Not only is he a sexual predator, but a cad, as well! THIS MAN MUST BE STOPPED!

D. E. F.—A VRWC

(Vast Right Wing Conspiracy) Operative

My Sexy Punishment From President Clinton A B&D And S&M Fable

Dear Special Prosecutor,

I never thought I'd be telling anyone this...but here goes!

In 1995, when President Clinton was up for re-election, my parents were very involved as fundraisers for the Democratic National Committee.

Consequently, they were thrilled beyond belief when they were finally invited to a special dinner to meet the President.

They managed to wangle an extra invitation for me, and although I'm pretty much of a libertarian and not too interested in Bill Clinton's brand of civil liberties, I knew that it was very important to my folks, so I decided to play along.

This meant that not only did I have to go to the dinner, but I had to act excited about it.

IT'S THE SEX, STUPID!

We arrived at the Four Seasons to find a red carpet and a brass band. Half the town had turned out to catch a glimpse of the Clintons as they arrived at the dinner. My parents quickly got caught up in political discussion with their friends, and I saw that I had a brief window of opportunity to sneak away and have a cigarette.

Actually, if I had just wanted a cigarette I could have pulled it out at the table, but I must confess that what I really wanted was a couple of hits from the big phat joint I had secreted in my pocket book.

I knew that the evening was going to run pretty long and that the speeches would be predictably boring, so I thought that if I could just get stoned, it would probably relax me enough to be able to smile the whole way through.

As I left the rooftop bar, I looked for the "exit" sign that would indicate a stairwell, which seemed like the best bet. The corridors twisted and turned and then I found it and ducked in. I hurriedly pulled out the joint and my lighter and was just getting into it when I heard a movement from down the stairwell...

I couldn't believe my bad luck - it wasn't just anyone, it was President Clinton!

His first words were "Young lady, I think you'd better put it out and hand it over!"

I was so nervous, I blushed bright red. I found myself apologizing and asking him not to tell, all at once in a sort of a confused babble. His stern expression began to twist into a smile.

"Young lady, you know that you are in deep trouble, don't you?" I looked down and nodded. "Do you think we should go find your parents?" he asked, smiling, "or would you rather that we kept this just between us?"

I looked up - was he going to give me a break? I couldn't believe it! I thought then and there that if he cut me slack I would vote Democrat for the rest of my....

"Well?" he asked.

"Just between us, please, Sir," I stuttered.

He looked thoughtful. "Somehow it doesn't seem quite right to just let this go...maybe I should just punish you myself?"

I felt nervous, but I trusted him, and I knew that I would never hear the end of it if my parents found out. Sure, they knew I occasionally smoked pot, but they would never forgive me for letting the President of the United States know!

I said, "What do you mean, Sir?"

He smiled and said that he thought that a good old fashioned spanking ought to do the trick. He took hold of my shoulder and guided me out of the stairwell. We walked down the corridor into a small private sitting room where there was a desk with a phone and a few chairs.

The President took off his dinner jacket and sat down in a straight backed chair. He looked stern as he told me to get over his knee. I guess I hesitated too long because he reached out and took my arm and told me "Get over my knee right this minute, young lady. I'm going to spank you within an inch of your life."

'Funny,' I thought. 'That's not what my father used to'....and then before I knew what happened he had flipped me over his knee, pushing the skirt of my dress aside, the slit in the skirt making it easy. I knew he saw the latex garter belt, and I started to blush. At the same time, I was starting to get pretty excited.

When the President pulled me into his lap, I felt his erection through his pants. He wasn't trying to hide it either.

He told me to put my hands behind my back, and when I did, he caught both my wrists in his left hand. With his right hand, he began to pull my panties down. Almost casually, his fingers brushed my vulva, and of course, came away wet and sticky. I felt his hard dick surge. He licked his fingers, then began to spank me, rhythmically and pretty hard.

I was getting really wet, and although I was trying to be cool, I kept wiggling against his strong thighs. Suddenly he smacked me much harder and told me to "be still". I froze. He pulled me up abruptly and told me to take off my dress, which I did.

Then he told me to bend over the desk and to spread my legs as far as I could. I felt totally exposed....

"Now, ask me to punish you. Say, 'please, Mr President, please spank me again'. Then, you will count and thank me for each one. If you forget, we'll start again. How old are you, young lady?"

"Twenty two, Sir," I whispered. "Then that is your number for this punishment."

I thought to myself, 'wow, I'll bet Hillary's ass really burns when she's bad'.

"Stick your ass out, baby girl!" I pushed my ass out. His strong hand on the small of my back held my wrists very tight, pressing me into the table. "Ask for it. NOW!"

I said "Please Mr President, please spank me again." His hand came crashing down. I couldn't believe how hard he hit me. I said "hey, that's too.." And that's when he slapped me and whispered in my ear that we could be here all night if I didn't behave.

Then he looked down at me and said, "If you want to make trouble, put your dress on and we'll go find those parents of yours."

Without a second thought I meekly said "Please Mr President, spank me again."

"That's more like it," he said, and once again, smacked my ass very hard.

IT'S THE SEX, STUPID!

In between the smacks, he'd rub my ass and my vulva. He pinched my butt and my clit, rubbing his palm in little circles. My ass was bright red and burning, and I was dripping wet. I couldn't believe how hot I was. In between the 19th and the 20th smack, he stuck a finger in my ass and a finger in my yoni.

I couldn't help myself, and I pushed back on his hand. He pulled it out, laughing, and gave me my 20th smack. He told me to get on my knees....

He stood in front of me, and pulled down the zipper of his pants. He adjusted his shirt tails and pulled his huge throbbing erection out. He told me to put my hands behind my back, then he cupped the back of my head in his left hand while he held his dick in his right fist.

I couldn't believe how big it was - really thick, glistening with pre-cum, with a head the size of a small orange.

"Do you want it?," he asked? I nodded. It was the most beautiful penis I had ever seen. Now I understood how he got to be President!

"Take it then!" I did. I wrapped my lips around it and he pushed down into the back of my throat. He began to fuck my face hard, making me take it all. It seemed to get even bigger. Then suddenly, he pulled me up and pushed me over the desk again. He grabbed me by the hips and ground his dick into my ass. As he did, he clapped his hand over my mouth, muffling the scream that was coming.

"Hold still and be quiet," he hissed.

I did what I was told. I was so wet that my pussy juice was running into my ass and his dick was still slick from my saliva so it didn't really hurt - it was more a feeling of being totally filled and controlled.

I felt the heat building in my belly and I whispered, "Please, Mr President, Sir, can I play with myself?"

He pushed my hand into my crotch and I began to eagerly finger my clit. Just as I started to come, he pulled out, and before I could stop him, he came buckets all over my face and breasts.

Luckily for me, there was a small lavatory adjacent to the room we were in. I got cleaned up and put my dress back on.

When I returned, he was sitting at the desk, looking thoughtfully at the joint he had taken away from me. "Now don't let me catch you breaking the law again, or we'll have to have another little session...."

I sure learned my lesson! I no longer break the law at public functions, and I always bring an extra change of underwear! Thanks for the opportunity to come clean, Mr Special Prosecutor.

Voracia Plenty

Austin, Texas

Snake Dance

He emailed me one night and said I need your services right away. The country needs you too. I need strength and inspiration. My work is great and I am only a man, would you come to The White House?

Of course I could not refuse my President's request, I E-mailed back and set the date. This was a special request, I planned and packed and informed his staff of my special needs to make the evening perfect. I called my costume maker for the finest silks to be made for me to wear for my President.

We were led to a room in the White House specially prepared for our meeting. silken, pillows covered the floors, the walls were draped in fine tapestries. The lights were large candles softly lighting the elegant room. Incense created the sensuous atmosphere. The music was perfect, ancient, Egyptian sounds of drum, and oude and bells and flute wafted throughout the room.

I was to dance for my President. He looked at me with a look I'll never forget. His eyes were soft and longing. His breathing was increasing, desire tensed his body. "Please, please," he whispered, "just dance for me."

And I began to move slow and soft, undulating slowly my skirts flowed as I removed my veils one by one slowly, slowly, touching him gently with their edges with each swirl and turn.

He lay back on the elegant pillows and sighed a sigh of deep longing. More he whispered, don't stop, please, just dance for me that's all I want.

I danced and danced, the quick staccato movements of my hips increased his breath, the subtle shimmer of my shoulders he loved, my head curved down to his as my hair brushed against his face, slow at first then faster and faster.

He lay back moaning almost crying. My heart opened full, my hearts energy went out toward his heart, and I felt the touching heart to heart. Open I whispered into the energy, open and receive dear president receive the love of woman open to the shakti, open, open, She will open you, allow, allow, allow, I whispered low and soft.

I reached into my basket and removed my serpent dance partner, a beautiful royal python named Osiris and we began our dance. Rhythmic undulations, hips shimmering, torso pulsing, Osiris wound up my spine contracting, releasing dancing me with his serpent body's knowledge.

Osiris reached my head resting his head upon my crown chakra, I received the shower of light from the crown of my head to the base of my spine, my yoni was ignited by the light, I breathed deep to hold the intensity.

IT'S THE SEX, STUPID!

I motioned for Bill to rise and dance with us. I held him in my arms as we swayed to the gentle sounds. Bill undulated and shook his hips pulsing gently and the look on his face was ecstatic. Osiris had wound around him, the serpents' head lying on his heart.

Suddenly, tears began to roll down his cheeks. I held his head to my heart and asked, "What is in your heart? Tell her, the Great Mother the desires of your heart."

He spoke, "My heart is so heavy, I wish to help the people of our United States and in turn help others around the world. We must see each other as brothers and sisters in this world as one. I am only a man I feel so inadequate, so alone. I did not take this office for myself for my own power and now I may not be able to do any good at all. I may fail." With that he sobbed from deep within his heart and I held him.

"Give this burden to her, to the Divine Mother and open to her." His look indicated that he did not understand. "Dance and feel deep into your body."

And, so he did, he danced and danced the serpent leading him into subtle, strong, deep movements. "I'm starting to burn," he said, "it feels so good." he breathed. His body began to shake, "I'm going to come!" he moaned.

"Hold this orgasm Bill!" I instructed firmly. I touched his scrotum in the spot that holds back the male orgasm firmly but gently. "Breath into it and pull the energy up."

He did so, breathing and quaking, breathing, deeper after each ripple subsided. I held each chakra between the palms of my hands as the energy undulated up his body and the serpent Osiris, held his spine, squeezing on each in breath and releasing on each exhalation.

"This feels so great." He spoke between breaths. "But it hurts, too. I feel that I'm giving birth when the pain hits my body, it hurts so much now. I feel like I'm giving birth!!."

"Yes, Bill you are giving birth to yourself."

He began to moan, and shake a quaking shaking that took over his whole body.

"What's happening?" He asked with fear in his eyes.

"It's The Divine Mother, Kundalini Shakti, Bill. Give yourself to her, open and receive her, the only way is complete surrender to her!"

"I can't he almost screamed. I'm so hard I have to come."

I held his scrotum again.

"Don't!" I commanded. "Don't miss this opportunity!"

He relaxed on that statement and asked. "What do I do?"

"Just breathe, Bill ask her to breathe you."

And she did, he breathed deep and long from his chest to the base of his spine. Each inbreath held longer and longer

73

each exhalation hissed like the great cobra serpent. The energy coalesced into his heart and he began to cry. "Oh, this pain is too great to bear. How, can I stop this."

"Don't stop, don't stop," I whispered into his ear, holding him close, pressing my body next to his, heart to heart I breathed with him. "Don't stop Bill, allow, allow, open, open, to her, receive her, surrender to her, open your heart, give her your pain."

And he did, at one deep breath he hissed the cobra's hiss, he moaned the pain of the world from out of his heart and cried out for her.

"Great Mother help me!" he cried.

And a great orgasm burst out from his heart. His whole body undulated in one full undulation after another. I held him through it all, after some time it began to subside.

He lay back on the silken cushions, his face glowing, his eyes full of light and satisfaction. He gazed into my eyes with the look of one who has gained wisdom, one who knows.

I kissed his forehead at the third eye, it pulsed, his third eye had been awakened and the crown of his head pulsed. We lay together cushioned soft by the silk of her love. I stroked his body and kissed his hair. He kissed me gently.

"Thank you." He said with deep reverence and respect. "I wanted this so badly but I could not say that I wanted it because I did not know what it was."

"And now you have it my dear Bill, my dear Mr. President. You have awakened the Divine Mother in your heart and she will lead you. Give your prayers and pain to her, and she will lead you."

It was time for me to leave. I felt great satisfaction yet my heart felt the separation. Of course, I may never see him again and be able to hold him close with my body. Yet, my heart will always love him. I pray to Our Divine Mother to lead and guide him always. I hold his vision in my heart.

May the power we hold as a nation spread it's blessings to the rest of the world. May we be able to receive the gifts of knowledge from the other great cultures of this world. May we live upon our Mother Earth in Peace and Harmony.

Om, Shanti, Shanti, Shanti

MyFillofBill

Dear Special Prosecutor,

Thanks to Mr. Bill Clinton, I have catapulted from a petite size 6 to a jumbo 18 in just six short months. None of my dresses fit and my feet are too fat for my shoes. I wander around in a bathrobe and a pair of thongs because I can't bring myself to go out and buy yet another wardrobe—and it's all Bill Clinton's fault.

It all started at the Dunkin' Donut shop in lower Manhattan. I was picking up a couple of dozen for the girls at work when a big, black stretch limo screeches to a halt outside the shop. Who streaks in but the President of the United States himself.

I could tell by the fire in his eyes that he and I shared the same passion: those luscious, honey-dipped babies that come piping-hot out of Dunkin's oven. Our eyes locked; it seemed like everyone else in the room disappeared; I knew I had to see him again.

I secretly followed the Presidential motorcade to its next stop: a Kentucky Fried Chicken. When Bill spotted me battling my way to the front of the line to be near him, he told an aide to bring me to his hotel room.

Twenty minutes later, I was led into a lushly-decorated suite where I found Bill surrounded by at least a half a dozen buckets of KFC chicken (the fried, not broiled kind). After a few minutes of small talk, I fell into his arms weeping, telling him how my 9-year-old pet hamster, Reggie, had just been diagnosed with a rare form of rodent cancer. I told him I couldn't afford the treatments anymore and that I was at wits end.

He consoled me with drumsticks, donuts, kisses and more. And now I'm hopelessly hooked. I slavishly follow Bill from state to state, and it's always the same thing: a late-night rendezvous with drumsticks, donuts, kisses and more. Then he goes home to Hillary.

Meanwhile I'm getting the ass of a city horse! Bill doesn't seem to mind the extra weight. He says it gives him more to love. But I sure as hell do. My life is a mess.

I have spent so much time chasing after that "creep" that I forgot to feed Reggie and he died. And it's all Bill Clinton's fault! You want me to help you get this guy? I'll wear a wire.

Distraughtfully Yours,

Mary Shaughnessy

The Jam Session

One of the perks of being a famous singer is getting to sing at the White House for the President and the First Lady. I've been there several times, starting when George Bush was in office. But nothing can compare with my visit last summer.

I was singing directly to the President, while gyrating my body about as much as I figured that stuffy audience could handle. It was pretty obvious that all it took to get him going was a couple of hot torch songs. So by the time I finished the set I could see old Bill was really getting steamed up.

Since I know a lot of musicians in Washington, we'd already set up a jam session later at the hotel where I was staying. So when I shook hands with the President in the receiving line, I bent over and whispered, "There's a jam session in my room tonight. If you want to come, bring your sax."

Well, an hour later he showed up at my hotel with his instrument in hand. When I opened the door, I could hardly believe my eyes. "No, Mr. President, I said bring your sax." I guess it was so noisy in the ballroom that night that he'd misunderstood. He looked kind of embarrassed for a moment, but after an aide brought his sax over, he joined right in and for a couple of hours he was just one of the guys.

When my friends all left about 3:00 in the morning, it was obvious that Bill was just getting warmed up. He poured us another drink, turned down the lights and turned on the radio. It didn't take a brain surgeon to figure out what else he wanted to turn on. But I was already there.

Holding my drink in one hand, I slowly unbuttoned my low cut blouse with the other, while crooning to the music on the radio. What a coincidence—the FM station just happened to be playing a song called "Touch Me" from my latest album.

As I put down my glass, I dropped my skirt and started swaying sensuously to the music in nothing but a pair of black lace bikinis. And then he reached for me.

The next two hours were a blur of passionate kisses, licking, sucking, teasing and the most delicious pleasure I've ever experienced. We jammed until dawn and when the session was over, he thanked me, packed up his instrument and silently stole away.

With no regrets…

Jennifer, the Juicy Jazz Singer

Deep Throat

Dear Special Prosecutor...

I didn't have sex with President Clinton, but I have information which sheds new light on the subject and will give your investigation a whole new perspective.

I am breaking vows and coming forward at great personal risk to tell what I know. The "I Had Sex With Clinton, Too!" cyber-protest calling for "confessions" will, I hope, provide me with both the cover of anonymity and a world-wide audience of millions. However, the price for revealing what I know in this way is that most people will think my "confession" merely an imaginative fantasy—that it isn't true. That's a chance I must take in the hope that somewhere out there are those who will read this and know that what I'm revealing is not fantasy but the truth.

Who am I? A Deep Throat. My identity must remain secret. There are those who will read these words and know that one of their own has broken the vows and betrayed them! And then my life will be in jeopardy. But it's a sacrifice I'm willing to make.

I'm not young anymore. And we all die sooner or later! What counts is what we do with our life! I cannot meet my maker with this on my conscience—knowing what I know and how, if it were made public, this knowledge would change everything! Many of the rumors surrounding the President's sexual liaisons are based on a profound misunderstanding....

The Presidency of the United States is the most difficult job there is. The most difficult job in the world! Leading a nation, leading a world, is the most responsibility a human being can have...more than any human can endure. And there is always a crisis, always the fate of the world is on your head. Shakespeare described how "heavy is the head that wears the crown." And so he deserves as much head as he wants.

Pardon the pun—a bit of on-the-job humor. What I mean is that the President is given "head" to lighten the burdens he bears. And it's not optional; it's mandatory. He has no choice. It comes (pardon the unintentional pun) with the job. The Secret Service realized that Presidents who don't avail themselves of these "perks of office" are a danger to themselves.

Those who hold the highest office in the land can't bear the constant and unceasing pressure. There is no day off, no time off, no respite...and always the weight of the world is on your shoulders. As our world shrinks, the President's responsibilities have grown. We've become a world community and the President, as the Leader, is responsible for more and more of it. So he wants out! But he can't get out! He's got four years of this "hell." Mind you, this is all unconscious. Consciously, he's as happy as a pig in shit!

So Presidents want out. But there's only one way out. And somebody out there in the ether picks up the message the President is unconsciously broadcasting into the collective unconscious of humanity. And then someone out there who is angry, unloved, feeling lower than low...some worm turns and with the squeeze of a trigger does the President a favor and brings the most beloved, the highest, the most powerful, the President down!

That is why my colleagues in a black section of the Secret Service are tasked with protecting the President by preventing his self-induced assassination. We protect the President from himself and his own unconscious, while the regular Detail protects him from some wacko out there who picks up his distress call.

Bottom Line…it's not just a job perk, it's a necessary therapeutic act, like massage, to keep the president from triggering an assassination attempt.

Throughout history kings, emperors, the leader, if you will, has always had "jesters," and "fools" whose job it was to make them laugh. Laughter on demand...because "heavy is the head that wears the crown." And these leaders not only had Fools and Jesters to make them laugh, but people to pleasure them, to give them head because "heavy is the head that wears the crown." And, by the way, so did the Queens!

Now about this Monica-business... She worked for us. She was following orders, protecting the president from himself. And the president? He was doing what he'd been instructed to do when he took the oath of office for his own safety and the good of the nation.

A Civil Servant with a Clear Conscience

I Feel So Cheap and Dirty...

Yes, I too had sex with Clinton. I have no book deal and only some fond memories. What brings me so much shame, though, is having sex with Starr. There, I said it.

I admit (as long as a big, six figure book deal is forthcoming) that I had great sex with Clinton...and also...to my undying shame, I had very, very boring sex with Starr.

I know I will be subpoenaed, my parents will be given the third, fourth and fifth degree, and that my book purchasing history will be laid bare for all to see, but I have been told that confession is the first step toward redemption.

Now, where's my money, and my free time-share private luxury cabin?

Not So Cheap and Dirty

P.S. I am so glad to see a place for those of us who are disgusted with the whole Inquisition-like atmosphere of the "special prosecutor" and the truly frightening array of forces who have made it their purpose in life to destroy the president (and with him, the presidency) ever since the fall of 1992.

It is as if they felt the White House was the private property of their party and their class. Thank you...and of course, all the above is meant in the spirit of good satire. After all, I have no desire to feel the whole weight of the "Special Prosecutor" bearing down on me....

Once was enough for THAT!

Love at First Sound Bite

Dear Ken Starr/Linda Tripp/Rush/Newsweek/Enquirer:

This is an actual, true confession of my real affair with Bill, a torrid intellectual/liberal scandalous affair!!

I first met Bill about seven years ago, when he was first running for President. It was love at first sound-bite.

I knew immediately I had to have him—those liberal views on healthcare, children, gays in the military—I was so excited, I could hardly contain my sex/intellectual drive. I often fantasized then about what having an intellectual conversation/caress with him would really be like.

You see, I am a male history teacher who usually prefers attractive women physically, but I have to admit to a secret lust for liberal ideas. I got hot in my pants just thinking about spending money for schools, and universal healthcare! Oh, I am getting hot again!!

Anyway, I told all my friends about him—the only reason the national media didn't find out is that Linda Tripp isn't a friend of mine.

I even went as far as working to get him elected, and even voting for him!! (Oh, will there be forgiveness for me somewhere in heaven...can my sins ever be forgotten...such liberal beliefs.)

It got even worse when he was elected—my fantasies grew and grew!! Oh, the sinfulness of it all—I actually believed our nation had rid itself of that Reagan economic idiocy of build more weapons and cut social spending and then lower taxes to create a bigger national debt—oh, yes, we were moving beyond that! The orgasms had no end!! The lust knew no bounds!!

But then it all crumbled—Newt had his way with us (a shameful affair, that—may God forgive those lusts also!!) and the conservatives realized that Clinton's ideas were working and dangerous, so they went after us, his affairs, his private lusts. Oh, the shame of it, may I burn in hell for thinking such liberal thoughts...heaven forbid we should seek to educate children better, to give healthcare to ALL young people...my sins are so great.

That is about it...I admit it is all true, and I am willing to testify before a grand jury—sorry, Bill, please forgive me, but I have a family to protect, and my students as well—they must be protected against such liberalism and caring about less advantaged people as you and Hillary (I am so jealous of her —a liberal wife who cares about helping the disadvantaged— Bill, how could you cheat on me that way and sleep with her ideas...).

IT'S THE SEX, STUPID!

So, that is my tale of woe and sex and fantasies and intellectual sin...I know I have done wrong, and I now seek a reprieve, let me find Gordon Liddy on the radio, then Ollie North—I, too can learn to screw the minorities and poor and children and handicapped and immigrants...just think of the lustful orgies of ideas we can come up with to screw all those wimps!

Mind-Fucked Left and Right!

Bob B.

Starr's In My Eyes...

Actually I would have had sex with the Pres but I am more patriotic than even thou. I choose to relieve the edge and crankiness with the Special Prosecutor.

Now I know why they call him "special." It wasn't your ordinary grill and cross examine ecstatic intercourse, it was more.

This is a man with a hard subpoena ready to enforce its will.

A whole world of fantasies evolved.

He could barely contain his excitement bursting forth discussing the pleasures of being handcuffed and his partners dressing up in stripes and going to a real jail. Just ask Susan McDougall he offered.

He said he would stop at nothing to get the goods exercising his manhood in ways no one could resist. He said he could bring any woman to screams of passion. The women just cry with pleasure at his Grand Jury foreplay he added. Truly he is a sexual addict and can't stop taking on all these women for his sadistic pleasure.

IT'S THE SEX, STUPID!

With his virility firm, taxpayers will continue to get screwed by him as the millions keep adding up. I am just breathless at his grasp and certainly won't reveal a thing about our intercourse, unless a good book deal comes as quickly as he does.

A Starr Fucker

In Case You Want to Subpenis Me

OK, well, this is a little embarrassing. And I didn't want to come forward but I hear that there is lots of money at stake, and maybe some famous Right Wing Republican might adopt 'lil 'ole me and get me a famous hairdresser and a makeover so I guess I have to do my patriotic duty and confess.

Plus, I know if I don't tell the truth, my dear old mammy will get brought before the Starr Chamber in chains and forced to answer questions about my underwear as a child.

And yes, I have shopped at Barnes and Noble and I guess they want to know about the books that I bought to drown the terrors that I have felt for years since the President first, well, uh...he first uh, well.

On second thought, I deny it all. Won't you please give me immunity Mr. Persecutor. Then I will tell all.

Everything you want to hear. Anything that might corroborate the thousands of others who have been victimized by this man and his now world famous member.

IT'S THE SEX, STUPID!

And Ken, if you don't choose to continue to waste our tax dollars and make us the laughingstock of the world, perhaps you would consider an offer to sell wieners in the Bronx. By now you must be an expert in them.

RAL

Making an Ass of Myself

I had sex with William Jefferson Clinton and I want the whole world to know about it! And I'm not afraid of making an ass out of myself.

It was during one of his vacation/campaign swings through the west that we met. He and Hillary decided they wanted to see the Grand Canyon and take a trip to the bottom (for you know Bill likes to get to the bottom of things).

I had been working at the Canyon just a few short months but during my tour, I had met a few celebrities and had gotten to know a few of them. I had more than one strong man wrap his bare legs around me and work up a hot sweat under the clear Arizona skies.

Well, let me tell you. When Bill saw me, he asked the tour guide if he could spend the afternoon going down on me.

My boss said, "Sure". He was the kind of guy who would do anything to please a popular president. So he gave me over to Bill.

IT'S THE SEX, STUPID!

In no time, Bill had straddled me and I let him wrap his legs around me for most of 4 hours. He enjoyed his visit to the Grand Canyon. And, it was the best time I ever had with any man. Mr. Clinton said he never a saw a more sure footed donkey.

So there, that's my story. I can tell the whole world and still feel like I didn't make an ass out of myself like everyone else who has had a story to tell.

Anonym-ass

Don't Let TRUMP & the GOP Sex-Scandal US Again!

IT'S THE SEX, STUPID!

Don't Get Sex-Scandaled Again!

The Clinton sex scandal taught us an important lesson: our sexual shame makes us easy marks for political manipulation.

The Clinton sex scandal of the late '90's held up a mirror, not only to our sexual hypocrisy but also to our sexual shame. During nightly newscasts, embarrassed anchors warned us of the graphic nature of their scandal coverage in a way they never had before. *("Warning: the following material may be unsuitable for young viewers"..."not for the faint of heart.")*

Where were these dire warnings during their coverage of wars, serial killers, or the O.J. Simpson double murder trial? If the President had been accused of murdering someone in the Oval Office, I doubt the media would have had such difficulty covering it or politicians discussing it. But to the American psyche, acts of sexuality were more shocking and taboo than acts of murder.

We may think that today, nearly twenty years later, we live in a sexually liberated society. Don't be fooled by our seemingly sex-obsessed culture. We're not liberated, we're just freer to express our sexual dysfunction.

One of the characters in my new novel, *The Secret Sex Life of Angels*, put it this way. "We live in a sex-drenched, sex-obsessed society. There's millions of porn sites online. Whatever kink or fetish you're into, you can find. So we're freer to express ourselves sexually. But that doesn't mean we're liberated.

"Why do all those *dirty* words get bleeped on TV? Because they're about *sex*! If we're so damned liberated, why is everything related to sex considered dirty? Calling them *dirty* jokes and referring to them as *dirty* words expresses the way we really feel about sex…which is that we're deeply ashamed of it.

"Sexual images are controlled—they're rated, censored, and even criminalized as indecent. Yet, our so-called *decent* society has no qualms about broadcasting the most horrible acts of cruelty into our homes. Meanwhile, images of a woman's breast or a man's penis are considered so immoral, so dangerous, so threatening to the fabric of our society that they have to be controlled. What does that say about our true feelings towards sex?

"Images of guns and knives, all the instruments of destruction, are everywhere, which tells our children that we approve of them. But God forbid they be exposed to images of our genitals—the instruments of creation. Why? Because the truth is that what we really carry between our legs is our secret shame."

The Clinton sex scandal taught us many things. Perhaps the most important is that our sexual shame makes us vulnerable to political manipulation. The shame we feel about sex is one of the levers those in power use to coerce and control us. It makes us easy targets for the psycho-sexual-political blackmail of a sex scandal. Real freedom means freedom from psycho-sexual-political manipulation. For that, we have to face our sexual shame and heal it. Until we do, we'll be vulnerable to being "sex-scandaled" again.

IT'S THE SEX, STUPID!

Afterword

It's my sincere hope that after reading IT'S THE SEX, STUPID! you will be protected against sexually-transmitted STDs— *Sex-Scandal-induced Thought Distortions*—and inoculated against the sex-scandaling manipulations of Donald Trump and the Republicans during this presidential election and beyond. Hopefully, we've learned our lesson and they can't screw us again.

— I. J. Weinstock, 2016

IT'S THE SEX, STUPID!

Postscript

The *"I Had Sex With Clinton, Too!"* petition of more than 500 confessions didn't stop the Independent Counsel's investigation or President Clinton's impeachment. Nor did it stop the political insanity. But it helped the people who participated retain theirs.

Besides organizing this act of political theater, I wanted to participate, too. But I wanted my "confession" to elevate not just titillate. At the time, I was trying to write a book about sex.

Flashback—A Deal with God

Four years earlier in 1994, I was sitting in the conference room of a law firm during a week of exhausting, mind-numbing depositions in a lawsuit that would determine the fate of the new cable network I'd created. As often happens in business, the big fish eat the little fish. As the creator, I was the little fish. My media partner and now adversary, a major cable network, was the big fish. I'd given the launching of my baby,

The Game Channel, everything I had. Now I was a David against Goliath, outgunned financially and outmaneuvered legally, fighting for my financial and creative life.

Sitting in that conference room day after day, surrounded by teams of lawyers, I must have zoned out and everyone else must have taken a break because suddenly I was alone.

That's when I heard the Voice. *"What will you regret on your deathbed?"*

I was stunned.

"What will you regret?" the Voice asked again.

My life flashed before me...

You'd have thought I'd have had lots of regrets at the age of forty-six. But only one emerged. And it surprised me. It was connected to a dream I'd had almost ten years earlier, a dream about sex. This wasn't your typical "wet dream" but rather a mind-blowing dream like the kind the biblical Jacob had about angels ascending and descending a ladder to heaven. In my dream, the angels were having sex!

The French philosopher, Teilhard de Chardin, conveyed something of the awe-inspiring majesty of my dream when he wrote, *"Some day, after we have mastered the winds, the waves, the tides and gravity...we shall harness...the energies of love. Then, for the second time in the history of the world, man will have discovered fire."*

When I woke up from that dream, I felt I'd been graced with a vision that I needed to share with the world.

But it was a daunting task to communicate something that was beyond words (about a subject as controversial as sex), and I soon got cold feet. Conveniently, I became distracted by more worldly pursuits. Alone in that law office nearly a decade later, I was surprised to discover that not sharing that dream was my ultimate regret.

So I said to the Voice, "Get me some money from this lawsuit and I vow to share my dream with the world." The lawyers returned from their break, the depositions continued, and I wondered if I'd been dreaming again.

In the real world it was a pretty safe bet that I wouldn't have to fulfill my part of the deal. The odds were overwhelming and I could almost hear the fat lady singing.

Yet, lo and behold, legal miracles occurred and the Big Fish found itself on the hook for tens of millions of dollars. Two weeks before trial they settled. Now I had some money and no excuse. It wasn't easy to walk away from Hollywood. But I'd made a contract, a soul contract. I'd made a deal with God.

My Confession—"The SeX-FILES"

Four years later, at the time of the Clinton sex scandal, I was still struggling—after several false starts that ended in shredded frustration—to find the right "story" for my dream.

As the *"I Had Sex With Clinton, Too!"* petition grew, I wanted to write a "confession," too. But I wanted my confession to offer another way to look at sex. If not a heavenly perspective, then perhaps an off-world one.

So I wrote the **SeX-FILES** (this was the late '90's!) as a "confession" from a female intelligence officer, who violates her oath of secrecy to exonerate President Clinton by revealing the details of our secret contact with Extraterrestrials. She describes how she (along with others, perhaps even Monica Lewinsky) was trained by the ETs to "deploy the President's antenna" and "sing the song" that would put him in contact with the ETs whenever he sought their counsel. Unfortunately, this ET communication technique resembled a "blowjob."

The Secret Sex Life of Angels

When I finally returned to my novel, I realized I'd found my "story." It was about a newly-elected president (no, he doesn't have contact with ETs) who discovers that to fulfill his oath of office he must embark on a sexual odyssey that could determine the fate of the world. Like all of his predecessors, he's briefed about a secret order that traces its roots back to ancient Egypt and the great goddess Isis. He's shown a parchment letter from the Founding Fathers urging future presidents, for the good of the nation, to be initiated into the *Mysteries of Isis* so they can glimpse the future in order to govern wisely. He's shocked not only to discover that many signers of the Declaration of Independence were initiates, but that initiation is sexual.

So I finally had my story. But life intervened. First came the heaven, then the hell.

Not long after I'd made my "deal with God," I left Hollywood and found Joy. We fell madly in love and were a match-made-in-heaven. The signs were everywhere—she was driving a car she called "Desiree" with a personalized license plate that read *JOYOUS 6*. And she had more than the usual interest in sex. A renowned astrologer who'd appeared on TV and eventually hosted her own local show, she'd written a book entitled, *DAYS AND NIGHTS FOR MAKING LOVE: Sexual Timing With Astrology.*

When I told her about my dream and the book I was going to write, she responded enthusiastically and wanted to help edit it. She believed that our society's attitudes about sex needed healing, and often told me that shining a light on this misunderstood area of our lives touched a deep part of her soul. So naturally we had to protest the sexual hypocrisy of the Clinton sex scandal.

From the moment Joy was diagnosed with breast cancer in 2001, our heaven turned to hell. I knew that our time might be limited, so I stopped writing so we could be together as much as possible. Faced with this life-threatening challenge, my book seemed unimportant. For the next six years, I dedicated myself to making Joy's life as fulfilling as I could. And I never finished my novel.

During that period, Joy often expressed regret that she'd consumed so much of my time and energy. Her illness, she felt, had been responsible for my not completing "our book." A couple of weeks before the end, she implored me to "finish the book." That was her last wish.

Now, thirty years after my dream, twenty-two years after my "deal with God," and nearly ten years after Joy's passing, I'm fulfilling my end of the deal...and Joy's last wish.

In a final irony, I'm publishing *The Secret Sex Life of Angels* while another Clinton, Hillary, is running for president.

About the Author

I'm the son of Holocaust survivors and grew up in New York and New Jersey. In high school I performed in musicals and became a football "hero" winning the Homecoming Day game with a 65-yard touchdown.

I've enjoyed a varied career in the arts—acting on stage, appearing in films, and even doing performance art on the streets of New York. While producing television in Los Angeles, I created a new cable network, The Game Channel, the precursor to GSN (the Game Show Network). I've also written several books.

Years ago, with my first wife, Daphna, I co-authored a groundbreaking book about women. *BREASTS: Women Speak About Their Breasts and Their Lives* (Simon & Schuster) was hailed by the Washington Post as "an important contribution" and the subject of an entire *Donahue Show* (the Oprah of its time).

In my recent memoir, *JOYride: How My Late Wife Loved Me Back to Life*, I described my year of grieving after the death of my 2nd wife, Joy. A remarkable thing happened—she began communicating with me from the Afterlife and led me on an incredible journey to heal my grief. Ultimately, like the final scene in the movie, *Ghost*, she found someone—a willing medium—through whom she literally loved me back to life. Had I not experienced it myself, I wouldn't have believed it possible.

Those sacred, sexual, supernatural encounters, which I call the *Rites of Joy*, occurred ten times during that year and helped heal my inconsolable grief. During these other-worldly sexual initiations, I was shown some of the secrets of human sexuality.

Books by I. J. Weinstock

IJWeinstock.com

FICTION:

- **The Secret Sex Life of Angels (Book I—*Mysteries of Isis*)**
  One hundred days into his presidency, Adam Hart discovers that to fulfill his oath of office he must embark on a sexual odyssey that could determine the fate of the world.

- **ULTRA BOWL**
  In this epic struggle between man and machine, an NFL football team is "time-napped" and transported 100 years into the future where they are forced to play against robots.

- **IT'S THE SEX, STUPID!** *Don't Let TRUMP & the GOP Sex-Scandal US Again!*
  A satiric look at how politicians use sex scandals to screw the public. Includes a sampling of the historic 1998 *"I Had Sex With Clinton, Too!"* petition, a prophylactic against sexually-transmitted STDs—*Sex-Scandal-induced Thought Distortions*.

NON-FICTION:

- **JOYride:** *How My Late Wife Loved Me Back To Life*
  (2011 eLit Award: silver medal for *Best Inspirational/ Spiritual Digital Book*)

- **Grief Quest:** *A Workbook & Journal to Heal the Grieving Heart*
  (FINALIST in the 2012 USA Best Book Awards)

- **The LoveSpell Secret:** *A 30-Day Heaven-Sent Program to Create More Love in Your Life*

- **Breasts:** *Women Speak About Their Breasts and Their Lives*
  (Simon & Schuster) by Daphna Ayalah & I. J. Weinstock

YOU'LL NEVER LOOK AT SEX
IN THE SAME WAY AGAIN !

THE SECRET
SEX LIFE
OF ANGELS

Mysteries of Isis

I. J. WEINSTOCK

The Ultimate Secret

In a world with no future, one man is offered a secret key from the past to unlock the greatest mystery of all.

One hundred days into his presidency, Adam Hart discovers that to fulfill his oath of office he must embark on a sexual odyssey that could determine the fate of the world.

The Secret Sex Life of Angels combines the intrigue and controversy of *The Da Vinci Code* with the spirituality and eroticism of the *Kama Sutra* in a fantastic saga about the sacred nature of sex.

"Every man needs to read *The Secret Sex Life of Angels*.
Every woman needs to have her man read this book."

"You'll never think about sex in the same way again!"

"This is the book everyone will be talking about."

**Find out more about *The Secret Sex Life Angels*
visit www.IJWeinstock.com**

www.ingramcontent.com/pod-product-compliance
Lightning Source LLC
Chambersburg PA
CBHW060522030426
42337CB00015B/1970